# A Town Like That

# A Town Like That
*poems*

Pat Mottola

GRAYSON BOOKS
West Hartford, Connecticut
graysonbooks.com

A Town Like That: poems
Copyright © 2024 by Pat Mottola
Published by Grayson Books
West Hartford, Connecticut
ISBN: 979-8-9907474-0-1
Library of Congress Control Number: 2024911685

Book and Cover Design by Cindy Stewart
Cover Photo by https://unsplash.com/@ToddTrapani
Author Photo by Isabel Chenoweth

# Praise for Pat Mottola's Poetry

Pat Mottola proves she is that rare poet who is a master of the portrait poem. She captures the idiosyncrasies, core, and heartbreak of each individual with a specificity that is electrifying. Pat Mottola is an absolutely mesmerizing and powerful poet.

—Laura Boss, author of *The Best Lover* and Editor of *Lips*


The poet's original and unbiased voice covers a wide range of humanity, surprising the reader from poem to poem. Pat Mottola's daring is uncommon. She makes the personal universal. She finds humanity on the raw edge.

—Michael Miller, author of *The Different War*


Pat Mottola's memorable poems cause us to remember people who might otherwise be forgotten. Mottola accepts humanity as it is. Through vivid detail, she creates a community of people whose lives are on the fringe of society. Mottola's poems will help keep the human fire alive as long as there is breath to sustain it because of her hard-won knowledge that what will endure is the human heart.

—Vivian Shipley, author of *The Poet* and *Perennial*

*to Vivian Shipley*
*my mentor, my friend*

# Contents

## III

I

# A Town Like That

I want to be a stranger in a town like that,
a town with a name like Red Lodge or Ike's Creek,
a town with more bars than people, a town where
the railroad tracks are always in your back yard
and the trains are just passing through—

a town where somehow everyone knows
who you are and all roads lead back to your last
bad dream, a town that you can never leave
because not even the Greyhound bus stops there
anymore.

# Room in Brooklyn, 1932

*after Edward Hopper*

I don't know where the spot of sun
comes from. It mocks the flowers that try
to save the dismal room—they soon will die.
Blossoms bent in unison will brush
the ghostlike vase that haunts the gloom,
taunting me as if

the past and future do not exist.
My rocking chair at rest, I think I might
stand up and walk away, but wishing
is immobile. Instead I stare through windows—
transparent walls that keep me on the verge
of nothing.

Outside, an old brick factory; it too
will soon collapse. Vacant as hope, it sprouts
like a hideous beauty, conceals a distant city
that shows no pulse, no sign of life—
as if it knows the flowers
are all wrong.

I am not lonely, not bored.
I have merely brought the Great Depression
inside. I hold it in my hands, turn
away from the light that invades my space,
wait for an epiphany.

# Almost Homeless

There are no homeless in this town,
but there's Annie. She walks
from Marbridge House on
West Main Street, pushes her cart
filled with bags and bundles,
her long-past-blonde hair trailing
behind, tied back with twine,
or sometimes a rubber band.
There is a curious beauty in the pluck
of her stride, the strength of her spirit
as she pushes on, thoughts adrift.
She talks as she walks uphill
to the Stop & Shop where she plants
herself near the bottle return
like a native flower
guarding her shopping cart
full of the salvaged empties
she saved from the street.

# The Man with the Briefcase

He walks early every morning,
crosses traffic at the intersection
of Route 70 and Main,
past the library across
from Saint Bridget's church—
some days a wedding, or funeral.

And mid-day to the south end,
past the Dairy Queen
and the Goodwill store.
Sometimes late in the evening,
he braves the north end of town
past the prison.

I know his distinct stride,
a sort of swagger,
as if he knows the way
to somewhere. Or nowhere.

I imagine he has a job.
No. Had one.
But still believes he has a place
to go. He wends his way
in all directions, all the time.

Sometimes on my walks
I pass him on Route 10,
say hello. He stares beyond me,
silent, as if he cannot hear
a human voice. Or won't.

He has a past. I think.
Doesn't everyone?
Some others in town call him
*Briefcase Guy.*

We each devise a different story,
invent a life for him,
label him with nouns and adjectives.
Mysterious. Misfit. Lonely

in his penny loafers
and blue button-down shirt,
clutching his briefcase
where, we suspect,
his true story lies.

# Mack

Mack lives above the liquor store
in the center of town. Mornings
he walks route 10 by memory—
the same path, repeated, timed,
each block measured in careful steps,
as he counts the bricks in the sidewalk
like Gretel's breadcrumbs. 180 bricks
to the town green, 290 to the synagogue
next door to the church, 345 to the cemetery.
When I pass him on my morning walk
he stops to talk, at high speed, his own eccentric
beat a song with one note, repeating
his own words like a refrain. Always
he asks if I go to church and where.
*If God is for us, then who can be against us?*
I don't tell him the truth, that I am a sinner.
I lie repeatedly as he repeats himself,
desperate to convince me I need salvation.
Rumor has it he's a broken genius
wanting to save someone. Maybe himself.
*Our faith can move mountains*, he quotes.
*For we walk by faith, not by sight.*
In 60 more bricks we pass by the gas station,
cars parked in the lot awaiting repair.
We part ways. *Bless you*, he says.
I follow my path home,
knowing Mack will find his own way.

# Gus

Giant
pockfaced
shadow
lurked
around town
in local hangouts
creepy
quiet
meek
but underneath
you knew
he was
hiding
something
you wanted
desperately
not to know about.

# Neighbor

After the new neighbor bought the house next door
she tore it down, the house on Maple Avenue
where Don and Denise lived for forty-four years,
raised their kids—the house with the manicured lawn,
Impatiens always in bloom encircling every tree trunk
in perfect pattern. Seasonal flags flew from the front
porch—daffodils, butterflies, autumn leaves—
then winter.

The first to go was the ancient magnolia
with the wrap-around wrought iron bench.
Then the front hedge. Next the porch; gone
the wicker furniture, the miniature fluted columns
that held up the ceiling where the American flag
flew and the hanging pots rocked back and forth
in a gentle wind.

The house itself was easiest, the wrecking ball
slaying plaster walls like Goliath, exposing the heart
of the vintage two-story structure, baring the upstairs
bedroom where young Michael and David had slept,
dream-catchers above their beds to ward off
monsters.

Not a twig left untouched—not the old
oak where the hammock swung, not the lilac
that scented the street in summer. And some
of my own, those impudent branches, intruders
that overhung her now-barren parcel of land
on Maple Avenue

to make way for her new fence, their roots
unearthed, dug up like useless artifacts
on Maple Avenue where, to the tune

of a backhoe—its song gone wrong—
years of history were erased like sidewalk chalk
after a storm.

# Father

I watch the old man with the walker
approaching ShopRite.
You follow behind him
like a shadow, close enough
that you can steady him
if he falters his steps,

perhaps the way he steadied you
on your first bicycle,
when you were five,
running behind you
until you finally took
off. Does he see you

now, the same boy,
as you become him,
wonder how you got here,
behind yourself, bound
to his slower pace?
You see his face in your mirror
each morning, silver in silver.

Inside the store you watch him
search the aisles, so many shelves
blank and empty. He nods,
as if to give a blessing,
as if you both know he will not find
what he is looking for.

# Zena at Eighteen

She worked at the flower shop
on Main Street in the old factory town,
the buildings crumbling brick by brick,
wondered why they hired her,
those spinster sisters,
who smelled like old Band-Aids,
who didn't trust her to ring up sales,
only let her dust
the figurines and glassware,
objects that sat on glass shelves
hoping for someone to touch them.
Each Saturday she went to Vonetti's for lunch
the cook licked his lips, told her she was
a real banquet. He would have let her
touch his cash register.

# To the Woman Wearing the Black Strapless Gown in Costco

Your hair is loose,
lips slicked, nails polished.
You ignore the smiles
and side-eyes as you glide
on your high heels through
aisles of produce, paper towels,
sample the foods of the day.
You wander by the rotisserie
chickens, catch the butchers
gawking at you as they carve
raw meat. Their stares
are delicious.

I know who you are.
You have no place
to go, nowhere to be.
Your last bad date
lasted too long, and here
you are, the morning after,
searching for something
in this place with so much
to offer, too many choices,
nothing you would want
to take home with you,
but good enough to try.

# When Tess Dropped Dead in Kmart

She didn't mean to embarrass her children,
the ones who shopped at Saks. Addicted
to the plastic bins, the blue-light specials,
enamored of the front-door greeter, she
couldn't help it. Home alone, she dreamed
of him, imagined herself on a date,
a private table in the Kmart Cafe,
eating Twinkies, drinking Kmart wine.
After hours they'd stroll through aisles,
create their bridal registry, discount
sheets and towels with tiny roses, flatware
matching Melmac plates and cups.
At midnight they'd make love beneath
the blue-light special blinking like a strobe
in a disco bar; then slow-dance,
smiley faces winking as her heart
throbbed. Her obituary bent the truth—
her children claimed her heart stopped
suddenly on her way to Bloomingdales

# The Dentist's Hobby

Troubled before and after
his ten years in the pen,
the dentist for whom
finding honesty
was like pulling teeth—
the molars, incisors,
taunting him with their clean
record. His office filled
with temptation, women's
breasts staring at him
like buck teeth, daring him.

And then one day he made
a new friend,
found a new hobby.
They stole some cars, filed
the vin numbers smooth
as veneers then sold them
hot off the block,
crafted a counterfeit title—
not the real thing, but
not quite false,
after all.

# Driving by the Meriden Pharmacy

Dubbed the "Silver City"
in 1876, you tarnished.
Gone is your silver lining;
your luster left along with
Napier, Remington Arms,
International Silver.
Stately mansions once
flourished, now in decay.
One airport, no planes; their wings
dissolved in the bitter winds
of time. And here you are, littered
streets, boarded-up storefronts.
and one drug store on the corner.
The sign says *Open*. Entrance
around the corner. The broken
parking lot threatening to swallow
what's left—the empty shelves,
bullet hole in the window,
statues of Mary on sale.

# Those Tombstones Are Breathing

Walk slowly. You can hear
their silent shallow breaths.
They are lined up in rows
in the hallways of nursing homes,
wheelchairs facing the courtyard
or the nurses' station, anywhere
but where they are, the corridor
of doom, their heads drooping
like daffodils in December.
Wilted, they talk to themselves
or to loved ones who
aren't there again.
Dry and wrinkled,
slumped in their wheelchairs,
these wounded warriors, no salve
to soothe them, no salvation.
More women than men,
though sometimes it's hard
to tell. So here they sit,
all brides and grooms
wedded to each other,
to the same hallway,
that long aisle of forgetfulness,
in their sleepy sameness,
a bond never broken
until death do they part.

# Epitaph, Hillside Cemetery

*As I am now, so shall you be,*
*Prepare thyself to follow me.*

I think of the dead
daily. Where they go when
they're gone, if they walk, as I walk
evenings, swiftly past these stones,
thin gray granite engraved with names
I never heard. Names.
Buried along with the dead.

Lucretia Brown, etched in place.
She died nobly, set ablaze
as she stoked the fire, cooking
over an open hearth, her bulk
of a dress kissed by cinders.
On her stone she is defined:
*Wife of Lemuel Brown.*
*Til death do us part.*

Tonight the moon is full.
I hear voices as I pass.
They call to me, whisper
secrets: flecks of silver
in the stone are souls trapped
inside; each full moon pulls
a female spirit upward.

II

# First Date

We walk for miles on the beach,
close to water's edge.
Bare footprints track our path
to mark our way back.
No seashells here, only stones.
You collect only the most perfect—
flawless, smooth and white—
contemplate a few,
place them in your pocket.
I feel their weight,
watch footprints disappear.

# On Second Thought

I don't believe in fairy tales.
Lies, lies, I realize.

The prince is the witch
in disguise.

I back down the aisle.
The limo driver opens the door

of my getaway car, speeds
me home in reverse

to undress, unveil.
My magic mirror

reflecting me,
single, free,

happily
ever after.

# Midnight

Such an incompatible pair, the 1 and the 2
side by side, the odd couple. See how the 1
stands rigid, stiff as the dead; he can't quite fit
the curve of her. Yet the pendulum swings,
ticks like a broken heart while the night yawns,
weary, chasing the morning for lack of dreams.

I reach to grasp your absence,
the quiet bursting in my ears
until one chime interrupts, rude like a two-year-old
tugging at my hand asking *where's Daddy*
and I close my eyes to the night, smell
the cigarette you left behind in your haste,
crushed and discarded.

# Never Get Married on Your Birthday

Don't
blow out candles
they are pretty
sticks of dynamite
that never warn
how easily
everything
could explode
sugar icing
in your face
doesn't make
it sweeter.

# Alice Speaks the Truth About Marriage

*...if one drinks much from a bottle marked Poison*
*it's almost certain to disagree with one sooner or later.*
*—Alice's Adventures in Wonderland*

A diamond ring—just another looking glass.
Wonderland—the perfect cure for boredom
until I mistake the White Rabbit
for a Knight; his world full of new rules
and rude creatures.

So I fancy the Cheshire Cat,
high in the spinning sky, climb the last
magic mushroom until I remember
nothing of where I've been or why
he wears that satisfying grin.

I drink and shrink
and grow and shrink again, never
find the key to anything, but there is comfort
in growing small. My dreams
disappear.

# Ode to Sephora

Like a high-class hooker,
you decorate every street corner.
Your neon lights beckon, seduce
me with your superficial beauty.
I can't resist your shimmer,
your mysterious scents that whisper
the promise of eternal youth,
call my name, and I tramp
willingly into your trap. I use you
up, then leave you like before,
just another painted whore
who steals your glow, knowing
it won't last until morning,
when I'll return, just like all the others
before me, hooked.

# Bar

He followed her in, pretending
to be sorry. She wasn't buying,
said she was tired of his lying.
He was already drunk, but not yet
alcoholic. She said she was leaving
as if she meant it this time,
the jukebox slurring songs
of love gone wrong,
songs she knew by heart.
It wasn't until after one more
martini he noticed her ring finger
missing the ring. Perfect circle
of white, showing what little they had
was over.

# Icarus

understood why I wanted
to touch him. He was hot
and he knew it. He promised
me everything under the sun,
then fell for someone else,
someone who melted his fickle heart,
scorched right through it.

# Ode to His Ex

She wanted
first his heart
then the ring
the big house
the country club
she wanted
a bigger ring
bigger boobs
a nanny
a divorce
and then
she wanted
his shirt
his kids
his pension
his soul
his bones
and everything
in between.

# She Wants to Warn Her Son

You'll find the wrong girl,
later wash your hands of her,
then rinse and repeat.

# The House We Live In

I don't remember why
we wanted it. The foundation
was weak. You say you didn't notice
the sawdust by our back door,
termites on the carpet, hungry.
That old house had cracks
in the ceiling. We never looked up,
forgot the maintenance was high.
We patched them with layers
of paint and excuses, didn't see
the harm in neglect.
Some people fix these things.
Some hammer the nails too deep.
We close our eyes, never talk
about it. Even a whisper
might bring down the house.

# When The Light Goes Out

The left wall is mine.
The antique dresser holds it steady.
Tucked inside the bottom drawer
my wedding ring lies in a box
like a corpse.

The right wall is his.
The bookcase filled with mystery novels.
Dusty pages fall apart,
beg to be rewritten.
No happy endings.

The wall between us,
strong, impenetrable, never speaks.
Like a stone fortress, cold and empty,
it listens to the silence and weeps.

# In Winter

Our long front lawn is glazed with fresh
snow, glossed over by a thinning layer of ice
that makes the surface shimmer in the sunlight
and covers the ruts in our lawn.

Across the street the neighbors play
with children, toss snowballs
back and forth, barely catching
breaths between the laughter.

Inside their home, warm in the glow
of fireplace, they embrace in the window,
oblivious to us as we stand still in the cold,
shivering beneath the icicles that hang

precariously from the pillars of our grand
mansion, dangling above us like stalactites
of Swarovski crystal, so far away
from the beautiful life across the street.

# Mrs. Dali Does Laundry

*after Salvador Dali,*
*The Persistence of Memory, c.1931*

She tells Sal a hundred times
*remember to empty your pockets.*
What she finds is surreal—
hotel keys, dinner receipts
for two outside of Madrid,
where she's never been.
He assumes *time will heal.*
She keeps the dirty laundry
inside, hangs him out to dry.
Hard objects become
inexplicably limp. If only he
thought to check his pants.

# Sunlight in a Cafeteria, 1958

*after Edward Hopper*

Don't think they might make conversation.
Her eyes, unsettled, don't know where
to look; they avoid the empty table
where salt and pepper shakers taunt her
as they couple together like man and wife.
Her back to the revolving door,
the sun's strong light annihilates her beauty,
as if the force of its glare is waging war.

Who will break the silence?

The empty polished tables wait for him
to notice her; instead he sits erect
in semi-shadow, holds an unlit cigarette,
hand half-raised as if expecting a match.
His gaze stares past her, thoughts outside
the picture frame, as if there is a chance
they will come to life, fully aware
they are only a work of art.

## Bad Barbie Reinvents Ken

Barbie, you always wanted to dump him,
replace him, extinguish the milquetoast
preppie Ken, the boring Ken, the Ken
who stayed home and fed his cats.

But Barbie, it's not like men were made
to be made over, back then. Only women.
Don't forget you were invented in 1959,
when women were not allowed to reinvent
themselves. Men did it for them and they
followed the rules like obedient children.

Barbie, not long until they picked on
your flawless figure, body-shamed your perfection.
But Barbie, you carried your baggage proud,
your skinny silhouette of strength.

Barbie, you knew what you wanted. A Ken
with energy. Your own perfect Ken. No sissy,
no pantywaist, no thigh-high shorts
or plaid shirts, no flip-flops, no cotton pajamas.

Girl, design yourself a Bad Boy with cowboy boots
and studded leather jacket. Hop on his Harley—
and get yourself one while you're at it.
Invent the Biker Ken, Drug Kingpin Ken,
Reefer Ken, Greaser Ken, the Ken
they would never make, the Ken who
will fall in love with the Barbie they can't
imagine, the Barbie you want to be—

Burlesque Barbie, Mae West Barbie,
Eve or Pandora Barbie. Super Barbie—
the Barbie you were born to be, collecting
those special Kens, loving them all

on your own terms, dressing and undressing.
Then send them packing.

III

# What I Wanted

I wanted her Fair Isle sweaters
in pastel colors that matched
her A-line skirts. I wanted her
pink sheets, the lace curtains
in her bedroom. I wanted her
parents—father in his business suit,
no factory worker on midnight shift—
mother who graduated from Brown,
no mom who cleaned houses,
took in ironing. I wanted her
father's silver Mercedes, not our old
Dodge Rambler with the push-button
starter—that square white box
that looked like our second-hand
Frigidaire. I wanted her oriental rugs,
not the worn beige shag in our living room
and hallway. I wanted fine china,
no Melmac, no paper plates even
on holidays. I wanted the antiques
and treasures her parents brought
back from trips to Europe. I wanted
her house, the one that welcomed
her friends. I wanted to run away,
to leave my old factory town.
I wanted. I wanted.
I wanted.

# Joey Jenks' Shoes

In Franklin School
I remember Joey Jenks
couldn't afford shoes. He shared
with his sister Laura; they took
turns coming to school, walked
from their bleak house on Burr Street.

I remember those shoes, scuffed
and worn, wondered if their seven
siblings before them had used
those shoes, wondered why
they were so poor, wondered
why his father didn't work
in the factory, like the other dads
in our old factory town.

I remember those shoes
were brown as rust, strapped,
like Mary Janes. I remember
they looked like girls' shoes
on Joey Jenks' feet. I wondered
if they pinched his toes.

I don't remember his clothes,
only those shoes. I remember
no one made fun of them.

# High School Reunion

I never go but I think of what I would say
to Billy McCarthy, who couldn't ask me out
because his mother said I was too Italian,
and I think of how no one cared about Jenny,
the girl who was picked on when *retarded*
was a vocabulary word and *bullying* wasn't,
and fat Josie Fein, whose father owned the
thrift store where everything was plastic
and made my eyes swell, and the girls who wore
the slutty black dresses to Senior Prom. I think
of how John Moore's father was the janitor
even though he graduated from Yale and how
we didn't know our favorite English teacher
was gay. How I wasn't popular because
my father worked in the factory
and how I wanted to be friends with D'Andre
because he was the only black boy in my white
school. And how my guidance counselor questioned
my father because of the essay I wrote in English class.
And how my best friend Karen was anorexic
before it became fashionable—her parents
thought our snooty school wasn't snooty
enough so they sent her to Miss Porter's
and then I visited her in the psych ward
in the dark and crumbling brick building
on Cedar Street and she showed me how
if she sucked her stomach in, she could put
her hands around her waist and touch fingers.
Then she died. I remember thinking that Donnie
Searles shouldn't have been dating
Carol Simmons, the pretty cheerleader,
but they got married anyway and then divorced.
I think how Judy Goldberg's house was the place
to go because her mom made TV dinners and when
I ran away from home I walked straight there.

And how girls weren't college bound, only
bound. Who knew the shy kids were brilliant
and the bold were insecure? Who would become
famous and who would die? Sometimes
I think how far we all have come and I wonder
who would come the farthest to remember
what we tried to forget. We all strolled the halls,
forgot our locker combinations—I still have dreams
where I'm late for class. And I think how no one
gave much thought to leaving high school,
or where we'd be in twenty or forty or sixty years,
never believing it would be right back here.

# Before Bobby Ulinski Got Fat

An only child, he lived
in the big stone house
on the corner of Homestead Avenue.
Each day Mrs. U would ask my mother

if I could come for lunch
so Bobby would eat.
I wasn't hungry but the toys
I didn't have at home looked delicious.

She fixed us pierogi, kielbasa, Kool-Aid
and cookies. She never smiled.
Sometimes Bobby and I would sit outside
on the swing in silence.

When his father came home from work
Bobby would cry. One day he up and left
the old neighborhood. Maybe he found
a place that would satisfy him.

Or maybe he'd just had enough.

# Liar

After you stopped calling, I searched
the Internet each week, googled
"obituary" and your name and town
and never found you. Like an oddly
recurring dream, relief and comfort
on awakening until the day I unearthed
you in the *Waterbury Republican*,
the cruelest Times New Roman font
claiming you were dead, your free spirit
now confined to a narrow newspaper column
that boxed you in like a coffin. I breathed
in your sketchy obit that didn't say much
of anything. I assumed it was the drugs
or the drink or maybe even the cancer
although maybe you made that one up.
But just in case, why didn't I call you,
as if I could have saved you from
Vietnam and Vicodin and vodka
and from yourself even if you wanted me
to. You were funny and smart and drop-dead
gorgeous but what kept me under your spell
was your mystery, the truest lies you told
so well; yes, the fairy tale prince was charming,
a Pinocchio with real flesh, soft hands,
narcotic lips that knew their way around a girl
like me who loved you in spite of all this.

# Letter to Private Bates

Turn off your expectations.
Use the remote if you must.
Turn off your identity—
you are not the same person
who left. Turn off the images
of your buddy's body
intact. You wear his blood
on your face. Splattered
like a rash.
       It itches.
             You scratch
with pills and booze,
the only friends you trust
to turn off your pain.
Turn off the battlefield,
the hush of the dead—
their silence reminds you
to never sleep
with your eyes closed.
Turn off the war inside
      your head.
           You want to
turn off reality.
You were only eighteen
reaching for that last inch
of life. It was too hard
to turn off the killing switch.

# Before He Did Cocaine

He used to be a soldier, strong,
protected our country, women
and children, his fellow soldiers, GIs,
enlistees who never signed up
for senseless slaughter in a strange
tangled jungle where all dreams end,
and then one day I caressed his face,
tried to flick some specks of powder
off his nose and he shrank back
as if my finger were a gun barrel
or maybe he was just a hero still—
couldn't help it—wouldn't let me
get a taste of what a real war was like.

# Running Through Grand Central Station at 1:00 a.m.

In haste, I chase the last train
out of New York City, my shopping bags
weighing me down as if I cleaned
out Bloomingdale's and Saks.
Inside the deserted train station
I sidestep the sleeping man propped
against the wall like a rag doll, the dust
and grime of the city his only possessions.
The sight of him in his tattered clothing
almost makes me miss a step.
Oblivious, he blends into the wall,
the floor, the urine-stained tile,
his homeless hands idle by his side.
I glance back briefly, keep going, leave
him behind.

# Letter to Mona

Mona, I saw you today in the Louvre.
You look so sad imprisoned there
since 1792. Obedient, you remain
in your frame, so small, Mona.
How did those men stuff you in?
Does it still hurt? Crush you, like a girdle,
squeeze you so tight your smile
becomes a wince?

In the museum we must whisper;
they think you cannot hear behind
the glass meant to protect you.
Mona, you are still seductive.
A curiosity, a puzzle, unsolvable,
always a piece of yourself missing.
Mona, you are everywoman.
Those men never knew you, never will.
You like it that way.

# Bubble Girl

*April, 2020*

April Fool's Day
has come and gone,
left behind its worst bad joke,
its cruelest punchline:
*COVID-19.*
I isolate, self-quarantine,
stare out my Victorian windows,
the antique glass exquisite
in the way it renders all things
magical, wavy,
distorted.
Today I don't recognize
the world I used to know.
Sidewalks empty
as classrooms, workplaces,
dreams.
Somehow I arrived here—
Nowhere.
The *new normal.*
Isolation, frustration,
determination.
I talk, text, Zoom
to an outside world
that welcomes no one.
I long to touch
but fear keeps me safer
than I want to be.
I am no match for
battling bacteria, viruses,
depression.
I am immune
to nothing, each air molecule
poison, every human
my enemy.

Like nonfunctioning T cells,
B cells, they will betray me.
Scientists found a cure
for bubble disease, *SCID*, but
here I sit, vulnerable
in my safe house,
my beautiful sad bubble,
my thin veil of security,
alone.

# To Those Born After My Death

*"As you are now so once was I..."*

I do not know you, though you walk
the earth above me. I feel your footsteps

through layers of soil and silt. You visit
those buried here beside me, anchored

under stones that bear their names. I sense
your presence as you move about, place

flowers on graves where bodies rot and only
bones remain. I eavesdrop on your conversations,

your regrets. I long to see your faces.
You do not know that deep within the earth,
I wait.

# Twelve

I was twelve. Our new house
bare. No furniture. No frills.
I wanted my bedroom to be lavender,
or orchid, as if something delicate
could live there, on Lambert Road.
Mama bought bedspreads,
scatter rugs, curtains – flowers planted
in this desert. My small portable stereo
played on the bare wood floor.
Full blast. Loud sounds
of Claudine Clark's "Party Lights"
filling the empty hallway
and sterile rooms with a teenager's
dreams
   of parties and party lights
   somewhere a happy place


but my father had PTSD.
World War II flashed in his brain
to the beat of an old 45,
a cheap stereo's unbalanced
arm bouncing and burning
grooves in black vinyl, the disc
spinning
   a girl yearning to be
   anywhere but here


it skipped and clicked
like a time bomb, my father's foot
a grenade missing the safety clip,
exploding the arm, the turntable,
Claudine Clark wailing through sharp black
shards
   like me,
   like me

and all these years later I am
still twelve knowing a man's touch
is a lead shoe, a combat boot,
battlefields sprouting
everywhere, trip flares singeing,
flashes of light singing in midair,
singeing and singing,
each song resembling
*Taps.*

# Séance

I don't believe
in spirits.
I don't believe
in life hereafter.
But my mother
is dead.
My sisters and I
gather around
the Ouija board
we found
in Mother's attic.
Here in the haze
of night
we light candles,
circle round, all
hands hovering
above the planchette,
and wait
for Mother's
incorporeal presence.
Rain smacks
against the window.
My memory floods
until I fill with tears,
until I am soaked
with her.

# Falcon Hall

*for my cousin, Walter*

In this smoky club
we frequent each Friday
after visiting our elderly aunts,
we reward ourselves
for our good deeds,
you and me, sit at the bar,
cousins chain-smoking
and chain-drinking.
It is three in the afternoon.
I picked you up in my white
and black convertible,
remembering the black and white
days, the photos of us
our parents snapped.
There we are in their '52
Chevy rag top, top down,
hanging out the window,
wearing white cowboy hats,
cap guns in our hands,
innocent times back then.
I show you a snapshot
I carry with me, our high
school years, me on your lap.
Remember how you took me
bowling, poked fun at my gutter-
balls and I laughed at how
I loved you. Days we'd spend
at Quassy Amusement Park,
cotton candy, roller coaster,
roller rink. Nights at the movies,
*West Side Story, Psycho,*
you held my hand at the scary parts.
And now we sit here, together,
in this basement bar where

time has stopped, wrapped us
in arms like minute-hands that won't let go
our childhood pleasures seeped through
scotch and Corona, filtered through the smoke
and haze of years gone by
and, dazed, we drink to a simpler time,
our glasses always full, then and now,
wonder how everything and nothing
has changed.

# About the Author

**Pat Mottola** teaches Creative Writing at Southern Connecticut State University, where she earned both an M.S. in Art Education and an M.F.A. in Creative Writing. In addition to working with students at SCSU, she is thrilled to teach both art and poetry to senior citizens throughout Connecticut. An award-winning poet and Pushcart Prize nominee, her work is published in journals across the country. Mottola is President of the Connecticut Poetry Society. She served as editor of *Connecticut River Review* from 2012–2017. On a global scale, she mentors Afghan women writers living in Afghanistan and beyond. A recent poetry collection by two of the women she mentored, *Maybe I Should Fly*, is published by Grayson Books. Mottola is the author of two previous poetry books: *Under the Red Dress* and *After Hours*. She was the recipient of the prestigious CSCU system-wide Board of Regents Outstanding Teacher Award in 2019, as well as the J. Philip Smith Outstanding Teacher Award in 2021. Pat Mottola is the inaugural Poet Laureate of Cheshire, Connecticut.

www.ingramcontent.com/pod-product-compliance
Lightning Source LLC
Chambersburg PA
CBHW060351130626
46553CB00003B/1182